A LOBSTER LESSON

Rolla Donaghy and Lynne Donaghy

DEDICATION

To agencies and groups that protect coastal and migratory
birds, fish, shellfish, marine life and their habitats.

The authors gratefully acknowledge the expertise and
supervision of Captain Tom and Helaine of Chatham Boat
Tours, MA, who made the summer adventure possible.

Early in the morning on the first day of an August visit to Cape Cod, three young boys are faced with endless ideas of fun things to do.

Where do the boys begin?

"Let's go fishing," says Frederick, with a yawn.

"I want to swim," says Calvin, eating toast.

"Hey, guys, it would be fun to have a race on the beach,"
says Jackson, looking for his sunglasses.

But the parents and grandparents have other plans.

"Guess what we are going to do today?" asks their mother.

"We will go on a boat," says their dad.

"Everywhere I look there are marinas with boats for fun and fishing.
I wonder which kind we will be on," says Frederick, eagerly.

At one of the docks, a Captain and his wife are waiting. The man
is the Captain of his fishing boat and his wife is his crew. The
Captain and his wife are experienced and knowledgeable.

Jackson asks them, "What can we do with the water
so deep, with the waves and high tide?"

The Captain replies,
"I agree that low tide
is better to swim, look
for shells and clams
and walk on the beach.
Right now, I am going
to check my lobster
traps. If your parents
accompany us, and you
wear life jackets and
follow all the rules, you
can help. A life jacket
is required for every
person on the boat."

The boat passes protected islands where wild birds play.

Ahead of them, the boys see a colony of seals, a group that
stays together to communicate, find food and shelter.

The seals appear cute, friendly and small, but when one rolls over, it is enormous!

A sailboat glides smoothly with the wind while the motor of the Captain's boat makes bubbles and froth in the water, called wash.

"There are many people fishing. How do you know which lobster traps are yours?" asks Calvin.

The Captain explains, "Every fisherman obtains a permit, correct
equipment, and a registration number. A marker or buoy with its
own colors and numbers floats on the surface, while rope attaches
it down to a lobster trap that sits on the floor of the bay."

"To keep dry, over your life jacket you can wear a fisherman suit,
because when water sloshes into the boat, everything gets wet,"
the Captain says as he hands them big rubber overalls.

"What do lobsters
like to eat?" asks
Frederick.

His father explains
that lobsters live
around rocks on the
bottom to find fish,
shellfish, and bits
of plants or algae.

Like being in a classroom on a boat, the boys watch, ask questions
and listen—until it's time for a hands-on experience.

Lobsters have sharp claws that pinch, and don't have elastic bands like the ones
in the supermarket. To protect their hands, the boys can wear thick gloves.

One boy catches the marker with a hook to find the rope to bring the heavy lobster trap to the surface. Frederick pulls and pulls as everyone waits to see what happens.

When a metal cage rises to the surface, the Captain explains how the trap works. The upper section is called a kitchen for holding shrimp or bait. If a lobster crawls in, it lands in the parlor and cannot climb out again.

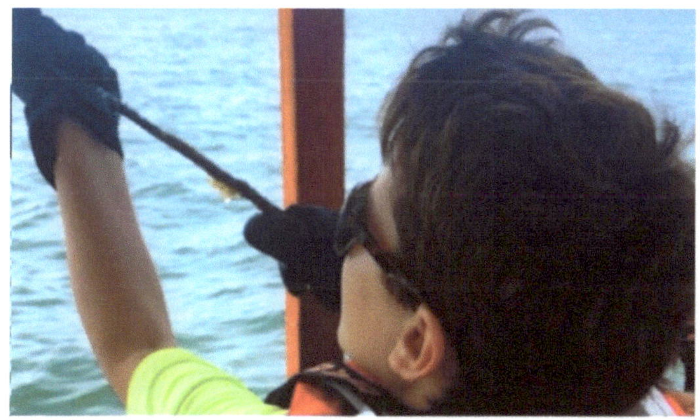

There are precise rules about fishing and catching lobsters. Each trap or cage must have an escape hatch for small things to leave, and a ghost panel with biodegradable ties that dissolve in case the cage is swept away or abandoned. A weak link near the marker breaks if a dolphin or whale is caught in the line.

"Can we keep this cute lobster?" asks Calvin.

"We can, only if it's the right size," the Captain says and demonstrates how to check the size.

The length of each catch is measured with a tool and unless it's the permitted size, it's returned to the ocean.

A female lobster with eggs goes back to insure there are lobsters
next year. If it has a special V notch, those are not kept. Very
big lobsters are left to keep the population hardy.

Catch, measure—that's the rule.
Release if it's small or too large.

The Captain says, "There were
no lobsters to keep there. Let's
go on to the next marker."

Of course, the bait attracts other creatures, and there are unexpected things
in the basket - wild crabs, small fish and a beautiful shell. The whelk is
a large snail with a fancy whorled shell, that lives on the sea floor.

"The whelk's alive, and I will put it safely back into the water," says Calvin.

The Captain removes a lobster to measure. It has 2 antennae and 10 legs, two of them being large claws, one bigger than the other. As lobsters grow, they molt, change their shell, and replace legs, claws, or antennae if needed. Jackson, wearing gloves, examines it.

"This one is long enough to keep," he says with a smile and places it in a bucket filled with ocean water.

"Only one lobster in each bucket," says the Captain's wife, "or they may start fighting. When there are three, we'll return to the docks."

As they return from the bay, the Captain's wife explains how to keep the lobsters wet, using newspaper dipped in salt water. She advises them to put a lobster on its back so it doesn't pinch or crawl away. The boys listen attentively and wrap the catch to put in the cooler.

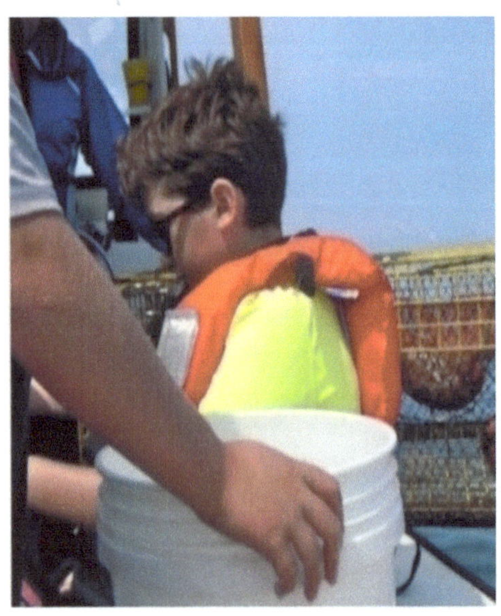

"I am wrapping mine in the sports section," says Jackson.

Frederick thanks the Captain, as Jackson returns the gloves, rubber
suits and life jackets, and Calvin carries the lobsters in the cooler.

The parents plan to cook the lobsters for dinner, just as if they caught a bucket
of fish. Not everyone can eat lobster, fish, shellfish, or peanuts, due to allergies.

The family talks about going to a Nature Center, or walking on the beach
together, perhaps at low tide to collect shells, swim and explore.

They leave behind the marina, the seals and a myriad of birds
that wait patiently for the fishing boats to return.

A lobster on display is easy to see.

A healthy, lively lobster prefers to be hidden in the rocks under the sea, not bright red but black, brown, yellow, orange and green to remain unseen moving around the stones, sand and algae.

EDUCATIONAL INFORMATION

Details about agencies that supervise the coastline, their public programs and visiting times can be obtained by contacting the service. Several that provided information relevant to this book are:

CAPE COD MUSEUM OF NATURAL HISTORY

869 Main Street, Rte. 6A Brewster, MA 02631 www.ccmnh.org

WELLFLEET BAY WILDLIFE SANCTUARY (MASSACHUSETTS AUDUBON)

291 State Highway, Rte. 6 South Wellfleet, MA 02663 www.massaudubon.org

CAPE COD NATIONAL SEASHORE (NATIONAL PARK SERVICE)

Park Headquarters: 99 Marconi Site Road Wellfleet, MA 02667

www.nps.gov

SALT POND VISITOR CENTER,

50 Nauset Rd. Eastham, MA 02642

PROVINCE LANDS VISITOR CENTER,

171 Race Point Rd. Provincetown, MA 02667

MONOMOY NATIONAL WILDLIFE REFUGE

30 Wikis Way Chatham, MA 02633

(US Fish and Wildlife Service) www.fws.gov

Note: Public access here is subject to restrictions

Lobster Exhibit photograph taken with permission: Salt Pond Visitor Center, Eastham, MA

Rolla Donaghy grew up in Canada where she studied music
and theatre arts. An educator in Toronto, Boston and
Honolulu, she has a specialty in reading development.

Lynne Donaghy has a business degree in marketing and has worked with
companies in Georgia, Florida and Louisiana. She enjoys spending time
with her children around school projects and outdoor activities.

The three boys (Liam, Kevin and Dylan) live in Minnesota with their dog,
Murphy, and their parents. They like to swim, play soccer, travel and visit relatives
who live in different places, including New England and near the Gulf of Mexico.

OTHER BOOKS BY
ROLLA DONAGHY
The Red of an Apple (YA)
The Perils of Pencil Lake (YA)
The Wind's Scrapbook

With Angela Amato (Beginning Readers)
Henry Hooper Leaves the Farm
Henrietta Hooper Chases a Starfish
The Picnic at Squirrel Park